The Church's
in the Book of Acts

Called and Equipped for Action

Daniel McGinnis

Principal, St Hild College

GROVE BOOKS LIMITED

RIDLEY HALL RD CAMBRIDGE CB3 9HU

Contents

Acknowledgments

This booklet is not specialist academic writing, though it is informed by serious study. It aims to help a wide range of readers engage with the dynamic story of the Book of Acts in an accessible way. I am grateful to students and colleagues at St Hild College who have offered feedback and helped to refine these ideas.

Note

All Scripture references are from the NIV except where noted.

First Impression June 2024
ISSN 1365-490X
ISBN 978 1 78827 xxx x

Introduction— The Church's Missional Purpose 1

A picture may be worth a thousand words, but a great story is worth a million. The Book of Acts is such a story, for its readers quickly find themselves in the narrative and see their concerns directly addressed in its many dramatic episodes. It continues to be relevant to many of the issues which the church is facing today, some of which will be mentioned throughout this booklet. The Book of Acts is also filled with stories of adventure and intrigue—shipwrecks, snake bites, miracles and dramatic legal showdowns make for memorable reading. But step back briefly and the reader quickly sees a theme which effectively unites these episodes: the unfolding of God's mission though his church. Acts is the story of the birth of the church in Jerusalem and its missional expansion throughout many of the urban centres of the Roman Empire.[1]

This story is partial and selective, as all history must be. Its author Luke focuses on the ministries of Peter and Paul and the growth of the church to the west and north, while mostly disregarding stories of the gospel going east or south. These are undoubtedly the regions and stories Luke knows best, and this illuminates another characteristic of Acts: it is thoroughly shaped by its author. This shaping reveals Luke's underlying purposes in writing his epic work and the influence he hopes it will have on its readers.

Luke is an historian and wants to be understood as a serious one

Luke is an historian and wants to be understood as a serious one; the preface to his gospel reads like classical Greek historiography, revealing the value he places on checking facts, finding reliable witnesses, travelling to obtain information and telling the truth as he understands it (Luke 1.1–4). However, ancient history was written not simply to communicate what has happened, but to instruct and influence its readers towards a certain course of action. This kind of persuasive speech is called rhetoric, and Acts is an excellent example of ancient rhetoric. Specifically, Luke is selecting and shaping stories from the past to inspire his readers to emulate Acts' heroes and avoid the path of its villains. The technical term for this is epideictic rhetoric, a common literary genre in the ancient world.

Acts is best understood in this way, and its repeated narrative themes of mission and church, which pervade nearly every episode, illuminate Luke's rhetorical interests. Luke draws on his sources to compile a narrative which seeks to inspire and equip his readers in their own missional witness. Jesus himself articulates this overarching purpose at the beginning: 'But you will receive power when the Holy Spirit comes on you; and you will be my witnesses in Jerusalem, in all Judea and Samaria, and to the ends of the earth' (Acts 1.8). This succinctly summarizes Luke's hope for his hearers, that like Christ's original hearers they will also receive the Spirit's power to be witnesses where they are, in the wider region and to the farthest limits of the earth. This is Luke's purpose in writing Acts.

After introducing this central idea, Luke goes on to present many of the missional practices and principles of the earliest church, in a vivid narrative written to inspire its readers and provoke them to missional action. There is nothing else like this in the NT or church history, which effectively links 'all that Jesus began to do and teach' with what he continues to do through the church (Acts 1.1).

Most scholars believe Luke writes Acts after 70CE, in a time when the great missionary leaders of the past have died, Jerusalem has fallen and Christ-followers are experiencing increasing persecution. The church has likely slipped into survival mode, losing the radical missional edge it possessed just after Pentecost. Luke is writing to remind his readers of the fiery early days of the church, confronting apathy and survivalism by painting a colourful picture of the earliest church in all its raw missionary fervour. The stories of Acts are meant to provoke, and they are not always comfortable reading. Its open-ended ending stresses that the mission which drives the earliest believers is not complete, but ongoing and urgent, for 'the ends of the earth' have not yet been reached. Luke persuasively urges his readers to join the expanding mission which Acts depicts so vividly. And he seeks to equip them in how best to do this, by telling memorable stories designed to prepare them to join in God's great mission to all nations.[2]

Luke writes Acts in an episodic fashion, which means readers need to pay close attention to the episodes which structure the story, including shifts in scene, characters, plot development and wider narrative context. Acts is the sequel to Luke's gospel, and they are written to be read together—each theme presented here will begin with an episode from the life of Jesus.

In this booklet, I present five key characteristics of the missional church in Acts and examine multiple episodes which underscore each repeated theme, showing how Luke has woven these ideas thoroughly into his narrative. I would suggest that the reader reads each episode in the Bible before reading my comments. My hope is that examining these episodes will provide new and illuminating insights and lead to a deeper understanding of why Luke writes the Book of Acts and what it means for the church's mission today.

2
Empowered by the Spirit

The first thing Luke wants his readers to know is that God has not left the church on its own to fulfil its missional calling. Instead, the great promise of the Book of Acts is that the Spirit will empower God's people to live this mission out.

Jesus' Baptism (Luke 3.21–23)

The Spirit's descent upon Jesus at his baptism inaugurates his public ministry. It is a trinitarian encounter, and the Father's words of love are a profound affirmation of Jesus' identify and sonship: 'You are my Son, whom I love; with you I am well pleased.' Luke implies that knowing the Father's love and pleasure is the foundation for Jesus' ensuing mission, which begins in the very next verse, and it is significant that this comes before Jesus has done any ministry and is simply based on their relationship as Father and Son. This is reemphasized on the Mount of Transfiguration, when the Father once again publicly honours Jesus as his 'chosen son' (Luke 9.35).

Luke is giving his readers an important insight into Jesus' fundamental motivation and resource for ministry—the Spirit is not merely an impersonal source of power for mission, but a doorway into knowing God's love and pleasure personally. Jesus' baptismal experience with the Spirit and the Father is a precursor to Pentecost, which echoes this foundational experience. This suggests that when the disciples later receive the promised Spirit, they also share in this identity of knowing themselves as dearly loved and chosen children of God, which is a fundamental aspect of the Spirit's empowerment for ministry.

Pentecost (Acts 2)

Jesus' pronouncement in Acts 1.8 should be seen as a prophecy and a promise—the Spirit will provide God's power to be his witnesses where they are and further afield. The immediate fulfilment of this promise comes in the great outpouring of the Spirit at Pentecost. This crucial episode is the decisive hinge on which Luke-Acts swings, for in Luke's gospel Jesus is the sole bearer of the Spirit after his baptism, yet from Pentecost the empowering Spirit is shared with all of Jesus' followers. Christ's life, death and resurrection make it possible, but Pentecost is the definitive turning point of not only Luke's story, but the wider story of the church throughout history. This is very much a trinitarian experience, for the Spirit is the Father's 'promised gift,' poured out by the Son (Acts 1.4–7; 2.33). Luke wants readers to understand that the church is born not of human effort or activity, but God's power.

The Spirit's role in Acts is to empower the church for mission, and this theme pervades the entire narrative. This pneumatology is distinct from other NT writings such as Paul or John—in Acts, the Spirit provokes missional action, protects the emerging church, takes hold of communities and is directed towards strengthening Christ's followers in their mission. Rather than explaining the Spirit, Luke shows the Spirit in action, presenting a compelling narrative character. At Pentecost, Jesus gives the Spirit to his followers to empower their ministry, including making the Father's love known personally to them, and the church is born.

The Jerusalem Church (Acts 2.42–47)

The Pentecost narrative underscores this missional connection—the story moves quickly from tongues of fire and mysterious languages to Peter's missional sermon. Peter presents this outpouring of the Spirit as the explicit fulfilment of Scripture, and even here its primary focus is missional proclamation to the multitude of nations gathered in Jerusalem for the Jewish festival of Pentecost (Acts 2.17–18; Joel 2.28–32). Many respond to Peter's message, believe, and are baptized, and about three thousand are added to their number (Acts 2.40–41). Yet dramatic as this is, it is not the culmination of Pentecost.

A careful reading of the Pentecost story shows that there is no narrative break until Acts 3.1, and therefore the mass baptisms lead directly into Luke's striking description of the early Jerusalem church (Acts 2.42–47). This is the climax of the Spirit's activity at Pentecost and illuminates a fundamental reality: in Acts, when the Spirit is poured out, the people of God are birthed and nurtured. The empowerment of the Spirit leads ultimately to the creation of a loving and unified community, God's church.

This earliest Jerusalem church functions as a prototype for Christian community and a standard against which all subsequent churches can compare themselves. Luke begins by saying they 'devoted themselves,' and this choice of devotion is the fundamental characteristic of the community. They willingly devote themselves to four things, which result in five further characteristics which only the Spirit can produce.

The Jerusalem church devote themselves to (Acts 2.42):

- the teaching of the apostles
- the fellowship (togetherness in community)

- the breaking of bread
- prayer

These focuses result in:

- a sense of awe in God's presence (Acts 2.43)
- signs and wonders confirming the message (Acts 2.43)
- the sharing of goods in community (Acts 2.44–45)
- a joyful sense of unity (Acts 2.46–47)
- people being added daily (Acts 2.47)

This episode is a profound picture of what the church can be, inspired by the devotion of its members and empowered by the Spirit. And Luke's final comment about the Lord adding daily to their numbers is a significant reminder of the church's ultimate missional purpose.

Ananias and Sapphira (Acts 5.1–11)

Shortly after this, Luke includes another summary passage about the church, further emphasizing their unity and generosity in shared community (Acts 4.32–37). This culminates in Barnabas as a positive example of the sharing of goods and flows directly into a negative example, in Ananias and Sapphira. This is a difficult passage, yet reading it in light of the Spirit's empowerment for mission yields some helpful insights.

Luke says their sin is 'lying to the Spirit,' which could also be translated 'they falsified the Spirit' (Acts 5.3). Their sin is arguably not simply lying or financial withholding, but falsifying the Spirit's presence in their midst in a way that violates the sacred fellowship of the community. The church has recently been birthed by the Spirit and any violation of its unity must be checked. This further demonstrates the Spirit's holy presence within the church in Acts, for it is fiercely protected and nurtured by the Spirit in its fragile and vulnerable early days.

This episode is not a repeated or normative pattern in Acts, and it comes at a unique and strategic point in the growth of the earliest church. But the Spirit's presence within and protection of the church is another example of God's empowerment for mission—the Spirit is committed to the purity of the church as a conduit for the advance of God's word. Luke underscores this by mentioning that as a direct result of this experience 'great fear / awe seized the whole church,' accompanied by many miraculous signs and wonders (Acts 5.11–12). This then leads to a further phase of missional growth fuelled by an explosion of supernatural healing (Acts 5.12–16).

Saul's Conversion (Acts 9.1–19)

Saul's encounter with Jesus on the road to Damascus is one of the most well-known stories in Acts, yet there is an ecclesiological dimension readers often miss. His experience of a blinding light and a voice from heaven are clear evidence of a theophany—this is a God-encounter. Understandably, Saul asks, 'Who are you?' and the answer is surprising, for Saul realizes that Jesus is God. Yet a closer look reveals something even more astonishing: Jesus says, 'Saul, Saul, why do you persecute me?…I am Jesus whom you are persecuting' (Acts 9.4–5). But Saul has not been persecuting Jesus, only persecuting his followers, his church. In this moment of double emphasis Saul realizes on a visceral level how deeply Jesus identifies with his church—to persecute them is to persecute him.

Learning that Christ and the church are one is arguably as foundational to Paul's calling and ministry as realizing that Jesus is divine. It sets him on a course to serve and devote himself not just to Jesus as Messiah, but to Jesus' church. It is no accident that from here Paul gives himself wholeheartedly to the church and goes on to establish and serve local churches for the rest of his life, as the theological extension of Christ himself. This must also be the foundation for his 'body of Christ' theology, which is unique to Paul (Romans 12; 1 Corinthians 12; Ephesians 4). This encounter vividly teaches him how personally Jesus takes the treatment of his people, and it is no coincidence that Paul goes on to become the most famous church planter in Christian history. The Spirit shows Paul that he cannot love Jesus without loving his church, and this empowers him to be 'God's chosen instrument' to the nations (Acts 9.15–16).

Guiding Paul's Mission

Most of the rest of Acts is devoted to Paul's missionary efforts, all of which flow from this confrontation with Christ and his church. It is notable how regularly the Spirit guides Paul in his mission. The Spirit instructs the church at Antioch, 'Set apart for me Barnabas and Saul for the work to which I have called them,' and Luke emphasizes this by saying they are then 'sent on their way by the Holy Spirit' (Acts 13.2, 4). It is difficult to overstate the significance of the Antioch church in Paul's wider mission, for this is the base which sends and receives Paul back throughout his missionary travels.

On his second journey Paul experiences another example of divine guidance (Acts 16.7–10). The Holy Spirit prevents him and his companions from going south into the province of Asia, and from going north into Bithynia, eventually squeezing them west towards the port city Troas. From here, Paul has a miraculous vision of the Macedonian man, which leads him to cross the sea to

Philippi and beyond. This spiritual guidance directs Paul across a significant geographical boundary and into his most fruitful church-planting ministry, in places like Thessalonica, Corinth and Ephesus.

Finally, Luke makes it clear that Paul's missional endeavours are led and empowered by the Spirit. On Cyprus, Paul is 'filled with the Holy Spirit' when he confronts Elymas (Acts 13.9). The disciples at Pisidian Antioch are 'filled with joy and with the Holy Spirit' as a result of Paul's ministry (Acts 13.52). When Paul lays hands on the Ephesian disciples 'the Holy Spirit came on them' (Acts 19.6). And when Paul is on his final journey back to Jerusalem, he is 'compelled by the Spirit' (Acts 20.22) and 'warned' by the Spirit about impending prison and hardships (Acts 20.23; 21.11). In all these references, Luke is emphasizing that Paul's mission is guided, empowered and sustained by the Holy Spirit.[3]

3 Welcoming Everyone

Luke's first message to his readers is one of reassurance—the mission does not depend on them, but on the power of the Spirit, who is available to support and sustain the mission at every point. However, his second message is a challenge—embracing God's mission means dismantling walls of division and exclusion and learning how to welcome everyone into God's loving family.

Jesus' Inaugural Sermon (Luke 4.18–29)

Luke's most cherished theological themes find their origins in Jesus' ministry in his gospel, and this is an excellent example. When Jesus stands up in the Nazareth synagogue and quotes Isa 61.1–2, he is summarizing his missional priorities, specifically that the Spirit has anointed him to minister to the poor, prisoners, the blind and the oppressed. Significantly, this is summarized as 'to proclaim the year of the Lord's favour,' and Jesus omits the next line from Isaiah, 'and the day of vengeance of our God' (Luke 4.19; Isa 61.2). Surprisingly, this beautiful message is not well received and even culminates in his listeners being 'furious' and outrageously attempting to murder him (Acts 4.28–29). How are readers to understand this?

Proclaiming the year of the Lord's favour is the key summary, and the word 'favour' is the word for 'welcome' or 'acceptance.' Some translators render this, 'to summon the inclusive year of the Lord,' or 'to declare God's age open and welcoming to all.'[4] Jesus emphasizes this by omitting the line about God's vengeance, which Jews would understand as a threat against foreign nations. Jesus further underscores this by proceeding to celebrate two examples of God welcoming and blessing foreigners (the Sidonian widow and Naaman the Syrian), in direct contrast to 'many' Jewish widows and lepers (Luke 4.25–27). Jesus is exposing the insular racism of his audience and challenging them to open their doors and lives to welcome all people, and this is what causes their violent reaction. This sets the scene for an extensive theme of universal welcome throughout the Book of Acts, where Jesus' prophetic challenge becomes directed towards the church.

Pentecost Revisited (Acts 2)

Pentecost is once again pivotal in the development of this theme. Luke reveals that Jews are staying in Jerusalem 'from every nation under heaven,' establishing a multicultural context for this important event (Acts 2.5). The holy city is inundated with pilgrims of many diverse ethnicities because it is the festival of Pentecost, and Luke goes on to list sixteen of these nations (Acts 2.9–11). This hints at Acts' all-encompassing emphasis—the gospel is for all people everywhere. While these are all presumably Jews or God-fearers (Gentiles drawn to Judaism), this episode sets the universal agenda in Acts: many different ethnicities hear the good news in their own language, in an anticipation of the wider mission to the nations which unfolds in the rest of Acts, and in fulfilment of key universal OT passages such as Isa 49.6 and Isa 66.18–19. This is emphasized when Peter declares to the diverse crowd that '*everyone* who calls on the name of the Lord will be saved' (Acts 2.21; Joel 2.32).

The Ethiopian Eunuch (Acts 8.26-40)

This colourful and influential character is most likely a Gentile God-fearer, interested in Judaism but excluded from full Temple worship. He is also a eunuch, and likely castrated, a clear exclusion according to Jewish law (Deut 23.1). He is a liminal character, in terms of his social and sexual status, and he is a foreigner from well beyond the borders of the empire. He is clearly seeking Jesus through the Scriptures, and his salvation and exuberant baptism are a direct fulfilment of Isa 56.3–5, about eunuchs being able to worship in the temple.

This moving episode, which is clearly God's initiative, shows the gospel reaching distant ethnic groups and 'the ends of the earth' actually seeing God's salvation (Isa 52.10). It is also about those who were previously excluded being included in God's people, which is why the eunuch goes on his way rejoicing (Acts 8.39). In a dramatic reversal, Luke is illustrating how Christ's salvation welcomes people who were barred from faith and fellowship. Additionally, it illustrates Luke's hermeneutical approach to the OT. He draws on a rich OT background, but selectively: he makes use of traditions which are universal and inclusive in scope (such as Isaiah, Joel, Amos, Genesis 22, Jonah), while disregarding insular voices which accentuate the rejection of foreigners and outsiders (such as Ezra, Nehemiah, and parts of the Torah).

Cornelius' Conversion (Acts 10.1-11.18)

Luke has been hinting at the church's mission including Gentiles, but the Cornelius episode is the pivotal point at which this becomes reality. Once again, this encounter is clearly orchestrated and endorsed by God, who paves the way with visions for both Cornelius and Peter. In Peter's enigmatic vision, 'Do not call anything impure that God has made clean' is repeated emphatically three times (Acts 10.15–16). It is difficult to overstate how many cultural barriers Peter breaks through when he steps into Cornelius' household, yet he faithfully begins to explain the gospel message to this Gentile family (Acts 10.34-43). As if to underscore that this is all God's initiative, the Spirit abruptly interrupts Peter's message and comes upon all who are listening while he is still speaking (Acts 10.44). Luke emphasizes just how shocking it is to circumcised Jews to hear Gentiles speaking in tongues and praising God, and in the ultimate affirmation of their Spirit-led conversion, Cornelius and his household are baptized (Acts 10.45–48).

Peter's reflection is telling: 'I now realize how true it is that *God does not show favouritism* but *accepts from every nation* the one who fears him and does what is right" (Acts 10.34, 35). Luke is accentuating the point that with God there is absolutely no favouritism, and that the Spirit is breaking down boundaries of prejudice, racism and exclusivism. The same Greek word for accept or welcome that Jesus used in his inaugural sermon is repeated here—this is the decisive point when the time of God welcoming everyone becomes a reality. And Cornelius is explicitly a 'foreigner' or 'outsider' in this story, 'welcomed' into God's family (Acts 10.28).

The focus of the story is not really Cornelius' transformation; in fact, it says nothing about how he or his family change, though we can presume they do. The focus is on Peter's transformation, so much so that perhaps this should be thought of as Peter's conversion to a new mindset. Through this experience, Peter begins to realize that his previous exclusive theological boundaries are being demolished by an all-welcoming God, who particularly includes the outsider. This is further emphasized in Peter's report back to the Jerusalem apostles: 'The Holy Spirit came on them as he had come on us at the beginning…So if God gave them the same gift he gave us who believed in the Lord Jesus Christ, who was I to think that I could stand in God's way?' (Acts 11.15–17). The primary leader of the early church is utterly transformed by seeing the Spirit come on Gentiles just as he had previously experienced.

Peter is utterly transformed by seeing the Spirit come on Gentiles

The Antioch Church (Acts 11.19-30; 13.1-4)

The momentum of Luke's theologically all-inclusive agenda is growing, and it is not coincidental that his next story involves a new church established at Antioch. There are multiple groundbreaking things about this church, including importantly that it is the first place where Jews intentionally reach out to Gentiles (Acts 11.19–21). This leads to the first multicultural church in Acts, which is explicitly affirmed by Barnabas (Acts 11.22–24). Luke presents this community as a model for overcoming difference and division and forging a new way to live as the unified and loving body of Christ.

This Antioch community is also dedicated to prayer, fasting and worship, and in this cauldron of spiritual devotion the Spirit speaks to them about sending Barnabas and Paul on mission (Acts 13.1–4). It is not an accident that this multicultural and boundary-breaking community becomes the launching pad for the next great phase of God's mission in Acts. The Antioch church is a strategic turning point, for here they do the hard work of managing difference, overcoming division and forging a diverse yet unified community, which leads directly to the commissioning of missionaries to foreign lands.

The Jerusalem Council (Acts 15.1-35)

The welcoming of Gentiles into Jesus' church is furthered in the ministry of Paul and Barnabas. Everywhere they go, they speak first to Jews, then to Gentiles. At Pisidian Antioch they explicitly justify this practice by quoting Isa 49.6: 'I have made you a light for the Gentiles, that you may bring salvation to the ends of the earth' (Acts 13.47). The Gentiles enthisiastically respond to this message, and believe (Acts 13.48). The practical and theological reverberations of this create an earthquake in a church with leaders who are largely stuck in an old mindset of insular exclusivism. This leads to an attempt to reconcile these differences and preserve unity in a fracturing church at the Jerusalem Council.

Luke presents the meeting of leaders in Jerusalem as a profound lived example of navigating difference and coming to a creative compromise that ensures ongoing unity and community coherence within the church. The question is not *whether* to include Gentiles, but *how* to include them. The solution takes the concerns of both sides seriously yet seeks to minimize the requirements placed on Gentiles. The challenge to the established Jewish majority is how to become tolerant, understanding and accepting of the other, the different, the excluded. Luke is holding up a vision of a church where believers of different ethnicities, backgrounds and social statuses come together in love to worship Jesus. The beauty of such a diverse and multicultural community is a goal worth striving for, for it glorifies God and presents a compelling witness. The Council's process and solution could be a helpful roadmap for many of the divisive challenges the church is navigating today.

Paul's Roman Ministry (Acts 28.17-31)

Emboldened by the decision of the Jerusalem Council, Paul continues actively to reach out to Gentiles throughout his missionary journeys, including before rulers while in captivity. His imprisonment eventually leads to Rome, where once again, we see his *modus operandi* of going first to the Jews and then to the Gentiles, for 'they will listen!' (Acts 28.23–28). In this context we find the final occurrence of Luke's central word 'welcome'—Paul '*welcomed all* who came to see him' (Acts 28.30). Here this concept of welcoming is applied as broadly as possible to everyone.

This completes a three-fold declaration about God's universal welcome:

- Inaugurated in Jesus' founding synagogue sermon, proclaiming the year of the Lord's welcome, particularly to foreign nations (Luke 4.19).
- Developed in the pivotal story about the welcome and conversion of the 'foreigner' Cornelius (Acts 10.34–35).
- Confirmed in Paul's Roman ministry of welcoming all (Acts 28.30).

This effectively bookends Luke-Acts and illuminates one of Luke's most cherished missional themes—the God of Israel is reaching out and welcoming all to join his loving family. This does not mean that Jews are any less welcome, for right to the end of Acts Jews are still being 'convinced' by the message (Acts 28.24), but it radically broadens the scope of God's salvation to include all peoples. For Luke, this is the original divine intention, first articulated when Yahweh promises to Abram that 'all peoples on earth will be blessed through you' (Gen 12.3). It is foretold throughout the Jewish Scriptures, and finally fulfilled in the ministry of Jesus of Nazareth and his Spirit-empowered church. By presenting this theme so compellingly throughout his narrative, Luke is urging his readers to also welcome everyone without exception as they take up the missional baton which Acts is handing to them.[5]

4

Sent and Sending

Acts depicts a missional church empowered by the Spirit and radically committed to welcoming everyone, everywhere. This church also understands its fundamental identity as being sent by God and grows to understand this as the basis for sending missionaries out to reach new areas and peoples. The root of the word 'mission' is the Latin *missio*, which means 'sending,' and is related to the Greek root of 'apostle' as 'one who is sent.' It is helpful to recall this fundamental meaning of mission, which is underscored throughout Scripture and church history. This theme emerges throughout Acts in a compelling way, which seeks to persuade its readers that they too are a missional people, both sent and sending.

The Sending of the Seventy-two (Luke 10.1-12)

Every missional initiative in Acts finds its origins in Jesus' paradigmatic sending of his followers on mission. The word 'send' is used three times in the first three verses of this passage, emphasizing that because the harvest is plentiful, but the workers are few, the Lord of the harvest is sending out workers into his harvest field. This missionary commissioning is theological and practical: Jesus sends them out two by two, to start with a house and search for a receptive 'person of peace' (Luke 10.5–7), and from there move to a wider missional focus on the whole town, healing the sick and preaching about the kingdom of God (Luke 10.8–11). Missional activity in Acts should be understood as an attempt to follow Jesus' missional instruction to his disciples. By intentionally mirroring this inaugural scene throughout Acts, Luke emphasizes that the subsequent Christian missionaries understand themselves to be sent by Jesus himself, faithfully following his teaching and expanding the outreach he began in Galilee and Judea.

Acts 1.8

It is crucial that Jesus' followers understand that his mission does not stop with his departure, but that the resulting outpouring of the Spirit will only accelerate it. The beginning of Acts focuses on linking the expanding mission that will follow with what has already been. Acts 1.8 is a christological promise about receiving the Spirit's power for witness, but it is also a geographical framework and chronological outline of the entire Book of Acts:

- You will be my witness in Jerusalem (Acts 1–7)
- And in all Judea and Samaria (Acts 8–12—the surrounding areas)
- And to the ends of the earth (Acts 13–28—Paul's missionary journeys move towards the rest of the known world)

In this regard, the whole of Acts should be regarded as the beginning of the fulfilment of Jesus' promise in Acts 1.8, all initiated by Christ himself. This is reemphasized as a divine command with identical language in Paul's mission: 'I have made you a light for the Gentiles, that you may bring salvation *to the ends of the earth*' (Acts 13.47; Isa 49.6).

Jewish expectations of salvation involve a gathering to Jerusalem, the spiritual centre from which they have always looked for salvation, and then a sending out from Jerusalem to the nations—Luke's gospel often mentions the centrality of Jerusalem in God's plan of redemption for the nations. At the end of Luke Jesus appears to the disciples, and 'opens their minds' by saying, 'This is what is written: the Messiah will suffer and rise from the dead on the third day, and repentance for the forgiveness of sins will be preached in his name to all nations, beginning at Jerusalem' (Luke 24.45–47). This saying holds together these tensions, maintaining the Jewish prophetic roots and importance of Jerusalem as the origin of the universal mission, while setting the stage geographically and theologically for the 'sent and sending' nature of the church's mission as it unfolds from Jerusalem to 'all the nations.'

Scattering (Acts 8.1-4; 11.19-21)

Filled with the Spirit, the early Jerusalem community grows rapidly in the first chapters of Acts, yet there is no hint of the predicted expansion into Judea and Samaria, much less 'the ends of the earth.' However, Stephen's martyrdom initiates a period of intensive persecution, which 'scatters' disciples throughout the wider region, and results in missional proclamation in Samaria and other neighbouring areas. This unplanned missionary expansion happens at the hands of 'all except the apostles' (Acts 8.1), and demonstrates the unfolding of God's plan, another of Luke's cherished theological themes. The implication is that even persecution brings about God's mission and widens its scope, which directly fulfils Jesus' prophetic promise in Acts 1.8. It also highlights the repeated theme of providential failure—in Acts, it is often great failure or crisis which brings about God's greater purposes. Significantly, these scattered evangelists end up at Antioch, where they begin to speak to Greeks as well as Jews.

Antioch Revisited (Acts 13.1–4)

Up to this point in the narrative, non-local mission has been unplanned and spontaneous, as people flee persecution or travel for other reasons. But the church at Antioch is the great turning point, the time when the church begins to realize it is not only a divinely sent people, but also a sending community. Luke presents this church as the prototypical sending church, for at the prompting of the Spirit, they lay hands on Barnabas and Saul and commission them for intentional missionary outreach into other locations.

This picture of a local church devoted to prayer and worship, responsive to the Spirit's leadership and giving up two of its central leadership team for planned missionary journeys to faraway places, establishes a paradigm for church-based sending and planting. For the first time in Acts, intentional non-local mission takes place, emerging directly from a worshipping community that is doing mission in its locale and wakes up to the reality that Christ wants to reach people in other places as well. In many ways, every subsequent mission trip and church planting endeavour throughout church history harks back to this pivotal Antioch episode, reminding God's people that they are a sent and a sending community.

Paul's Missionary Journeys (Acts 13–21)

Luke devotes the next nine chapters of Acts to Paul's missionary efforts, which originate from and return to Antioch in ever-widening circles. Luke presents these journeys as paradigms for mission, and the repeated themes reveal the key strategic approaches Luke is emphasizing.[6] It is notable that Paul almost never travels alone, and that his goal in a new destination is always to establish a house-based community of Christ-followers as an entry point for further outreach to the town or city, and never to leave converts isolated. Paul follows the Spirit when such spiritual leadership is clear, but he is also pragmatic—he follows roads and shipping routes, existing networks of relationship, and is prepared to change his plans when persecution breaks out.

When Paul is considering a potential location, he looks for urban centres with synagogues and begins with a Jewish or God-fearing 'person of peace,' who receives his message and opens wider social networks to his teaching and influence. He relies on miracles as supernatural confirmations of his message. Note the many similarities with Jesus' foundational missional instructions (Luke 10.1–12). Paul continually preaches about Jesus, adapting his message to be contextually relevant to his hearers. He is happy to move on once a beachhead is established and leaves the embryonic spiritual community to carry on in local witness, while supporting them through multiple visits, written correspondence and appointed local leaders. Eventually, many of these communities grow into citywide and even regional networks, and a linked web of Pauline coworkers and churches scattered throughout much of the Roman Empire emerges.

Paul's missionary travels are remarkably successful—in a period of about 13 years Paul begins at least 14 new churches, many of which develop into important centres of early Christian worship and mission which impact their wider regions. The repeated details of Paul's missionary exploits reveal what Luke is rhetorically encouraging his readers to imitate.

Ephesus (Acts 19.1-21)

Paul plants many important churches during his travels, including those at Philippi, Thessalonica and Corinth, but the climax of his missionary activity is in Ephesus. The majority of his third journey focuses on this urban capital of Asia, and he spends a remarkable three years ministering there. As is his custom, Paul begins in the local synagogue, but is soon presented with an exceptional opportunity to use the 'lecture hall of Tyrannus' for long-term daily instruction (Acts 19.9). An explosion of supernatural encounters happens at Ephesus, including extraordinary miracles being done at Paul's hands and his work clothes being used to heal many, the sons of Sceva having a humiliating encounter with a demonized man, and many publicly renouncing devotion to sorcery and burning magic scrolls. The Spirit is powerfully at work during Paul's Ephesian ministry.

The Spirit is powerfully at work during Paul's Ephesian ministry

Dramatic experiences such as these transform the heart of Ephesus itself—the fabric of the local economy is so fundamentally altered that the silversmiths and related tradesmen riot because their business has been disrupted. Luke emphasizes the sweeping results of this citywide ministry—'The word of the Lord spread widely and grew in power,' so much so that 'all the Jews and Greeks who lived in the province of Asia heard the word of the Lord' (Acts 19.10, 20). Luke is claiming that the missional eruption in Ephesus has a massive regional impact, and implying that every population centre in the province of Asia hosts a viable local gospel witness.

We know of one example of this regional impact, for Epaphras is trained in Ephesus, sent to plant the Colossian church, and is then leading outreach to Laodicea and Hierapolis, two towns in that immediate area (Col 1.7–8; 4.12–16). It seems that like Epaphras, many local church planters are trained and sent out from Ephesus into key population centres throughout Asia, leading to the establishment of many of the well-known early churches in this region (Revelation 2–3). The strategic importance of this Asian ministry is highlighted in

Paul's climactic emotional farewell speech to a significant group of Ephesian church leaders gathered at Miletus (Acts 20.13–38).

Luke highlights churches to serve as prototypical models of certain communal attributes he is advocating in Acts:

- The Jerusalem church exemplifies generous, devoted and unified Christian community (Acts 2.42–47; 4.32–37).
- The Antioch church typifies multicultural community and a devotion to God's presence that results in the intentional sending of its members to faraway places (Acts 13.1–4).
- The Ephesian church demonstrates the ultimate transformative impact that a local church can have on its city and wider region (Acts 19.1–20).

Through Paul's sustained training and sending ministry in the capital of Asia, all of this huge geographical area hears the good news of Jesus Christ. Luke's hope is to inspire his readers to dream this big and to convince them that they too, like Paul, are both sent and sending. The ultimate result of this could be the transformation of not just communities, not even whole cities, but entire regions and nations.

5
Willing to Suffer

The mission of the church is the prominent theme of the Book of Acts, and Luke shapes this through nearly every episode. But a closely-related narrative motif is suffering and opposition. This is so prominent that many have proposed that Luke means his readers to think of Paul more as a prisoner than a missionary. However, this is a false dichotomy—Paul's suffering and imprisonment are very much a *part* of his mission and they serve to further his outreach to new audiences. In all of Luke's stories of persecution, including Paul the missionary-prisoner, Luke is seeking to prepare and instruct his audience in how to respond to their own missional suffering. He paints a striking picture of a church willing to suffer sacrificially on behalf of the mission.

Jesus' Prophetic Predictions (Luke 21.12–19)

As is always the case, this theme originates in Jesus' teaching and example. This important passage functions to prepare Luke's readers for the suffering and imprisonment coming in Acts and beyond. It predicts the impending persecution, the legal trials that will follow, the unique empowerment for testimony before kings and rulers, the betrayals and martyrdom that will befall some, and God's ultimate protection. Importantly, Jesus summarizes this sort of suffering as 'an opportunity to testify' (Luke 21.13, NRSV). This clearly articulates Luke's fundamental paradigm: for Christ's followers persecution is a unique and strategic opportunity for witness. This is emphasized in multiple other places in Luke's gospel, including Luke 12.8–12 and Luke 6.22–23.

Before the Sanhedrin (Acts 4.5–22; 5.27–42)

The twin Sanhedrin trial episodes are the first instances of persecution in Acts, and both provide an example of how to respond when on trial. Their common themes relate to boldly testifying about Jesus to captors and viewing trials as opportunities for missional proclamation. They significantly invert honour and shame expectations by claiming that anyone undergoing persecution should rejoice because they have been found worthy of suffering disgrace on behalf of Christ's name (Acts 5.40–41). Through these stories Luke is teaching that suffering for the name of Christ is an honour and a central part of the missionary calling, public trials are opportunities for bold witness (Acts 4.20; 5.42), followers of Jesus must obey God rather than people (Acts

4.19–20, 5.29), and opposition will not ultimately hinder the spread of the gospel (Acts 4.29–31; 5.39).

There are other episodes which reiterate these themes, including Stephen's death, in which he is presented as the ideal Christian martyr (Acts 6.8–7.60). When the believers are scattered, this ironically brings about the expansion of the word and the activity of Hellenist missionaries throughout Samaria, Damascus, Phoenicia, Cyprus and ultimately Antioch (Acts 8.1–4; 11.19–21). Even while fleeing persecution, these faithful disciples continue to proclaim the gospel. In all of these episodes, Luke's main message is about how persecution can lead to new missional opportunities for those with eyes to see and the boldness to act upon them. As always in Acts, suffering is not antithetical to the mission but facilitates it.

Paul's Suffering Prior to his Jerusalem Imprisonment (Acts 9.15–20.12)

Luke uses multiple characters and situations to make his point about mission and suffering, but Paul is his ultimate example. Just after his conversion, Christ speaks about Paul's calling and finishes with an ominous prediction: 'I will show him how much he must suffer for my name' (Acts 9.15–16). From this summary, Paul's mission unfolds with a comprehensive array of opposition and suffering. He is forcibly expelled from six cities and seems to attract mob violence like a magnet. His experience in Lystra is particularly vicious—the violent crowd stone and leave him for dead outside the city (Acts 14.19–20). After being revived he leaves for Derbe, only to return quickly to Lystra (Acts 14.21). Here Paul is the model suffering missionary, a heroic example for Luke's readers to imitate in comparable situations.

The imprisonment of Paul and Silas is another important episode (Acts 16.22–39). They are severely flogged, beaten with rods and left in stocks, yet their response is to pray loudly and sing hymns of worship to God. The resulting earth-shaking deliverance and response of the Philippian jail keeper and his household are evidence of divine approval. This scene functions as consolation, reassuring readers of God's presence and protection in fearful times of suffering and opposition and challenges readers to respond with a similarly vigorous faith. Once again, Luke demonstrates that imprisonment is an extraordinary opportunity to proclaim the gospel boldly.

Paul's Captivity and Trials (Acts 20.13–28.31)

As Paul makes his way to Jerusalem at the end of his third journey, he receives multiple predictions of impending suffering and imprisonment (Acts 20.22–24; 21.4, 11–14). These are fulfilled when he is taken prisoner and begins a new phase of his ministry, incarcerated and on trial, but still very much a courageous missionary. This involves at least five significant opportunities for missional proclamation to diverse audiences, before the Jerusalem crowds (Acts 22.1–29), the ruling Jewish Sanhedrin (Acts 23.1–10), the Roman governor Felix (Acts 24.1–27), Felix's successor Festus (Acts 25.1–12) and Festus and King Agrippa (Acts 26.1–32). All of these are direct fulfilments of Jesus' earlier prophetic words (Luke 21.12–19).

While the precise details of these public trials vary, their common themes are instructive, and illuminate the actions Luke is advocating. First, Luke sees trials and imprisonment as ideal platforms for missional proclamation and understands suffering on behalf of Christ and his mission to be an honour. Christians who find themselves in similar situations should boldly proclaim Christ's message, defend themselves vigorously in court using every advantage at their disposal, and emphasize their personal story, trusting that God will give them the words they need. Above all, missionaries should recognize God's presence in their suffering, whatever form it may take, and trust that he will intervene on behalf of the gospel and its messengers (Acts 18.9–10; 23.11; 27.23–25, 34–36). Christ's presence is the strength and reassurance a suffering missionary needs, and his vindication will ultimately materialize, even if this means dying well for his sake.

Christ's vindication will ultimately materialize

Acts presents a comprehensive roll call of situations of persecution and suffering: when imprisoned and on trial, when threatened with immediate death, when scattered by threats, when undergoing the threat of mob violence, when stoned, when in long-term captivity, when under house arrest and even when threatened with a natural disaster such as a storm and shipwreck or a natural danger such as a snakebite. These stories provide both strength and training to their readers, as well as an overt challenge to imitate Paul and others in their responses to such situations. The message is clear—Christ's people possess a primary missional vocation, and suffering is a central and unavoidable aspect of this calling. Willingness to suffer is fundamental to what it means to be the church and follow the Spirit's leadership.[7]

6

Relevant in Every Generation

The 'Ending' of Acts (Acts 28.30–31)

Scholars have long been befuddled by the way Acts ends, or perhaps it is better to say the way Acts does not end. Luke has been building towards the conclusion of Paul's mission and has hinted four times that Paul would appear before Caesar, so the reader looks forward to this confrontation, and learning how Paul's life and mission will resolve (Acts 25.11–12, 21; 26.32; 27.24). Yet none of this materializes in Acts, and Luke does not even describe the outcome of Paul's impending trial in Rome. How are readers to understand such an unsatisfying conclusion? Perhaps Luke is planning a third volume? Perhaps he writes as Paul is on trial, and does not know the outcome?

The way Luke ends Acts is an intentional literary strategy

I would propose that the way Luke ends Acts is an intentional literary strategy—the narrative does not end because the mission does not end, and Luke is attempting to persuade his readers to carry on the missional story which he has begun. The rhetorical effect of this is clear—the church's great mission to all nations, begun in the life, death and resurrection of Jesus, amplified at Pentecost and furthered through Paul's ministry, is ongoing to Luke's day and beyond. The overarching promise of Acts 1.8 that Christ's witnesses will reach the ends of the earth remains unfulfilled, for if anything Rome is 'the centre of the earth,' and certainly not 'the ends of the earth.' The ending of Acts is a rhetorical device designed to hand the baton on to the readers of Acts, that they might take their turn in God's unfolding mission, acting in continuity with these earliest Christian missionaries and churches.[8]

Acts has a remarkable ability to draw its readers into its dramatic story—the vivid missional episodes make for compelling reading. And by abruptly departing from the ongoing storyline, leaving multiple narrative details unresolved and questions unanswered, Luke is essentially presenting an unfinished story to his readers and saying, 'Over to you now.' The final verse is a significant description of Paul's ministry in Rome: 'proclaiming the kingdom of God and teaching about the Lord Jesus Christ with all boldness and without hindrance' (Acts 28.31, NRSV). The last word of the book, 'unhindered,' speaks of the way that the gospel is continuing to spread, and Luke is urging his readers to also proclaim the kingdom and teach about Jesus boldly and unhindered, in their own time and context.

The Message and Relevance of Acts

The way Acts ends is an important indicator of its message. We have seen that mission and the church are the primary repeated narrative themes in Acts. But this story is not merely an ancient historical account, of interest to those who want to understand the origins of the church. Instead, so many of the details of how the church engages in mission are meant to be normative for church life in every age—Luke tells these stories to inspire and equip his readers to follow in the footsteps of the heroes of faith he describes. And by leaving the story unfinished, he emphasizes that the mission begun by these earliest disciples carries on in every generation, until Jesus' promise of 'the ends of the earth' being reached is fully realized. Ever since Luke wrote Luke-Acts, the church's mission has echoed and built upon these first stories which Acts so strikingly presents.

There is an immediacy to many of the stories in Acts—we read them and cannot help comparing the experience of the first disciples to our own experience of church and mission today. However, it is not always straightforward to translate these stories into contemporary application. The world of the Book of Acts is vastly different from the myriad cultural contexts of the modern world, and so implementation requires significant contextualization. This process revolves around understanding the trajectory of missional practice in Acts, and then imaginatively tracing this arc onwards to today. The contemporary church cannot naively mimic the exact practices it finds in Acts, but must discover its own innovative practices, doing the challenging work of reflection and contextualization, while using Acts as a helpful and inspiring guide for this crucial journey.

The contemporary church must discover its own innovative practices

Acts has inspired the church in mission in every generation since it was written, though with varying degrees of popularity. During Christendom in the West, Acts largely fell out of favour, for it describes a minority church that is prophetically impacting culture from the margins, and when the church has become the established majority voice, the radical missional stories of Acts seem much less relevant. However, much of the West is increasingly post-Christian, and the church is looking for new ways to engage culture missionally. Culture is also broadly post-enlightenment, and perhaps more open to the spiritual and supernatural about which Acts speaks so frequently. I would suggest that the Book of Acts is exactly the guide that the church requires today. Its themes of diverse and multicultural church, of overcoming division, opposition and suffering and of loving and bold outreach have a surprising resonance with today's cultural confluences. Christ's church has the potential to be a prophetic voice of service, leadership and influence today, and the narrative of Acts can help to show the way.

Where Do We Go from Here?

I am convinced that the missional adventures and intrigues which Acts describes are not merely historical particularities, but that Luke presents them as models to be followed by his readers. And I continue to wrestle with questions surrounding the missional patterns Acts depicts and their relevance to church life and witness today. What exactly readers do with this material will vary widely from one context to another. This makes contemporary application difficult to specify, though it is hoped that the following reflections will be helpful.[9]

The patterns and practices of Acts should inform the church in every age: things like the missional energy and focus, cultural sensitivity in sharing the good news, commitment to unity and relationships, bold proclamation, prayer, self-understanding as sent and sending and the welcome of everyone are fundamental to what it means to be and to do church. Some parts of the Acts narrative are more contentious, such as the emphasis on miracles, visions and angels, the practice of sharing goods within community, and even the particular way the manifestations of the Spirit occur at Pentecost and elsewhere. Readers must grapple with all of these repeated themes, certainly not quickly dismissing them, yet different streams of the church will come to different conclusions about their relevance and application. Despite this, it seems to me that Acts gives five clear invitations to the church today, as it depicts a missional church that is:

- *Empowered by the Spirit*—The mission is God's, and he gives the church all that it needs and more to carry it out. This involves knowing the Father's love and pleasure, as well as guidance, protection and miraculous power to carry the mission forward. Acts invites today's church actively to pursue the empowerment of the Spirit for mission, remaining open to all that this might mean without putting preconceived boundaries around it. The same Spirit that came upon the church at Pentecost and throughout Acts is still fuelling the mission's progress in a multitude of diverse and creative ways.
- *Welcoming everyone*—God's loving family is open to everyone, no matter their background, ethnicity, social status, location or anything else. This total inclusivity inspires Christians to carry and

communicate the gospel to all people, everywhere, and to create diverse communities of loving acceptance. Today, the church is invited to consider the challenging question of who the outsider and excluded are and ask for wisdom and courage to find ways to welcome them into community. This posture of generosity and openness will be crucial as Christians navigate complex moral and cultural questions in the future.

- *Sent and sending*—The fundamental identity of the church is that it has been sent from God on mission, and by extension it is empowered and called to send its own missionaries to proclaim the good news of God's love. Today, the church must reflect on this twin identity of being sent and being a sending community. How can believers respond to this sent and sending invitation in their own missional context, recognizing that the church exists for the mission, and not *vice versa*?
- *Willing to suffer*—The church in Acts understands that there is no price too great to pay on behalf of God's unfolding mission and consistently sacrifices its own comfort and security to continue to spread the message. Today, the church can ask God for grace to embrace discomfort and pain in its journey of discipleship and mission. This may mean navigating difficult relationships and rejection, or it may be something much more severe, but the Western church's passivity and resistance to suffering is a great hindrance to its radical missionary vocation. Acts invites the church to find God's purpose in pain and follow Christ and early Christian leaders in their model of sacrificial love, no matter the cost.
- *Relevant in every generation*—The church's mission as described in Acts applies in every generation and this invites us to do the important work of contextualizing it for our own situation in faithful and imaginative ways. How is God calling Christ-followers to take their part in the continuation of the great but incomplete story begun in Acts, and carried through every generation of the church to today? How can you take up the missional baton which Acts is offering you?

If we take these invitations seriously, I am convinced that we shall find all the missional inspiration and equipping that we need and more in Acts. After all, the mission belongs to God, and he will enable his church to answer this call to missional action and compose the next chapters of this grand story of redemptive love for the whole world. Let us respond with faith and wholehearted joy, for the sake of our neighbours and the ends of the earth.

Further Reading

There are many excellent studies of the Book of Acts which explain much of the background information and narrative analysis required to more fully understand these rich and complex stories. Here are some of my favourites:

D Bauer, *The Book of Acts as Story: A Narrative-Critical Study* (Grand Rapids, MI: Baker Academic, 2021).

R Gallagher and P Hertig (eds), *Mission in Acts* (Maryknoll, NY: Orbis, 2004).

J Gonzalez, *Acts: The Gospel of the Spirit* (Maryknoll, NY: Orbis, 2001).

C Keener, *Acts: An Exegetical Commentary*, 4 vols (Grand Rapids, MI: Baker Academic, 2012–2015).

D Marguerat, *The First Christian Historian: Writing the 'Acts of the Apostles'* (Cambridge University Press, 2002).

D McGinnis, *Missional Acts: Rhetorical Narrative in the Acts of the Apostles* (Eugene, OR: Pickwick, 2022).

M Parsons, *Acts* (Grand Rapids, MI: Baker Academic, 2008).

D Peterson, *The Acts of the Apostles* (Grand Rapids, MI: Eerdmans, 2009).

J Proctor, *Acts of God: The Message and Meaning of the Book of Acts* (Grove Biblical booklet B 49).

A Robinson and R Wall, *Called to be Church: the Book of Acts for a New Day* (Grand Rapids, MI: Eerdmans, 2006).

B Witherington, *The Acts of the Apostles: A Socio-Rhetorical Commentary* (Grand Rapids, MI: Eerdmans, 1998).

N T Wright, *Acts for Everyone*, 2 vols (London: SPCK, 2008).

Notes

1 A helpful introduction to the message and meaning of the Book of Acts, including key themes and issues, is J Proctor, *Acts of God: The Message and Meaning of the Book of Acts* (Grove Biblical booklet B 49). Ian Paul's recent Grove booklet summarizes *The New Testament's Vision of Mission* (Grove Mission and Evangelism booklet MEv 138). Many helpful commentaries discuss the key issues in Acts scholarship, including C Keener, *Acts: An Exegetical Commentary*, 4 vols (Grand Rapids, MI: Baker Academic, 2012–2015), B Witherington, *The Acts of the Apostles: A Socio-Rhetorical Commentary* (Grand Rapids, MI: Eerdmans, 1998) and D Peterson, *The Acts of the Apostles* (Grand Rapids, MI: Eerdmans, 2009). I am indebted to the insights found within each of these commentaries.

2 My book *Missional Acts: Rhetorical Narrative in the Acts of the Apostles* (Eugene, OR: Pickwick, 2022), is a much more in-depth analysis of the missional content of Acts.

3 See McGinnis, *Missional Acts, op cit*, pp 28–43 for more on the empowerment of the Spirit in Acts.

4 D Balch, 'Luke-Acts: Political Biography/History under Rome. On Gender and Ethnicity,' *Zeitschrift fur die Neutestamentliche Wissenschaft,* 111 (2020), 82.

5 See McGinnis, *Missional Acts, op cit*, pp 44–70 for more on the Father's universal offer of salvation.

6 See McGinnis, *Missional Acts, op cit*, pp 147–246, for more detailed analysis of the missional content of Paul's journeys.

7 See McGinnis, *Missional Acts, op cit*, pp 247–294, for more on missional suffering in Acts.

8 Many early commentators recognized this, including John Chrysostom: see M Parsons, *Acts* (Grand Rapids, MI: Baker Academic, 2008) p 366.

9 Many works make further connections between the church's mission in Acts and today, including R Gallagher and P Hertig (eds), *Mission in Acts* (Maryknoll, NY: Orbis, 2004); J Gonzalez, *Acts: the Gospel of the Spirit* (Maryknoll, NY: Orbis, 2001); A Robinson and R Wall, *Called to be Church: the Book of Acts for a New Day* (Grand Rapids, MI: Eerdmans, 2006).